CFA Level 1 Stu

By: Josh Wilkinson

Disclosure:

The author and his work are not affiliated and are in no way endorsed by the CFA Institute, CFA Program or any of its affiliates. The author does not guarantee any exam results pursuant to reading and reviewing the following selection of formulas and notes. While concise and helpful, the following formula guide is made to be just that (concise and utilitarian); in that, there may or may not be formulas or other required materials not disclosed in this guide and just because a formula, term, or study topic is included in this text, or any that are excluded, does not preclude that these are the only areas of study or that they are the only areas on the exam; in fact, it is possible some of these topics and formulas may not show up. It is your responsibility as a candidate to discipline yourself and prioritize your study efforts.

In short, I'm me and not an entity affiliated with or endorsed by CFAI or the CFA Program and reading through and reviewing this guide alone is by no means a complete and effective way to prepare for the test. As you continue to progress through your studies, you will continue to happen upon formula after formula and nuance after nuance. The purpose of this guide is to allow you to focus on the underlying context of the material and provide you with a collection of formulas, terms, and study tips that will reduce your time making lists and compiling and provide you with a concise form of review.

Introduction:

This guide is designed to be utilitarian (a quick guide which you can skim to read through a particular topic area or a find a specific formula). As such, each formula, term or tip is to be found following its specific test area. For example, if you are in need of a formula concerning probability, it can be found under the categorization, "Quantitative Methods". I hope you find this a useful tool to aid in your study efforts. I created this because as I was pushing through the material, I couldn't find anything similar to this within a reasonable budget. Being an eBook, this guide is portable on your devices, laptop, and can be stored in your cloud. You need not worry about index cards, pieces of paper, or randomly assorted sticky notes. Good luck in your efforts! – Josh

The topic areas, or chapters, follow this sequence: Ethics and Standards of Professional Conduct (including GIPS), Quantitative Methods, Economics, Financial Reporting and Analysis, Corporate Finance, Portfolio Management,

Equity Instruments, Fixed Income, Derivatives and Alternative Investments.

Ethics and Standards of Professional Conduct

While ethics and standards do not warrant the intense memorization skills needed to recite statistics formulas, they do warrant a great deal of study time as they consist of 15 percent of the entire Level 1 exam. This topic also comes back, to a lesser extent, in the following Level II and Level III exams.

While I can provide no one-size-fits-all solution for answering ethics questions, I can equip you with the same tools I've used. The Code of Ethics consists of six components. Verbatim, from the CFA Institute, is this list, the Code of Ethics, that should guide not only your conduct, but your understanding of how the capital markets operate on trust and instill in you the ideas of self-regulation and development of a core professional integrity.

The Code of Ethics (CFA Institute):

   Act with integrity, competence, diligence, respect, and in an ethical manner with the public, clients, prospective clients, employers, employees, colleagues in the investment profession, and other participants in the global capital markets.

Place the integrity of the investment profession and the interests of clients above their own personal interests.

Use reasonable care and exercise independent professional judgment when conducting investment analysis, making investment recommendations, taking investment actions, and engaging in other professional activities.

Practice and encourage others to practice in a professional and ethical manner that will reflect credit on themselves and the profession.

Promote the integrity of, and uphold the rules governing, capital markets.

Maintain and improve their professional competence and strive to maintain and improve the competence of other investment professionals.

Investopedia claims that an excellent way to learn the ethics material is to learn the following pneumonic: PEJMAR.

P is for priority. The clients come before your employer, who comes before you.

E is for encourage. Encourage or promote others to build repute for the industry and to act professionally. It is encouraged you introduce the Code of Ethics to your supervisors.

J is for judgment. Utilize your best judgment and care when dealing with clients and investment decisions/ recommendations.

M is for maintain. Upkeep current records. Have your notes and analyses handy.

A is for act. Act with integrity, be diligent, and act and effuse confidence that reflects well upon you, your peers and the industry.

R is for rules. Play by the rules. Not doing so reflects poorly on you, potentially the CFA Institute, your peers, and the entire industry. Trust is important and a loss of trust in capital markets is hard to regain.

The Standards of Practice Handbook is available on the CFA Institute website in the form of a free PDF.

I suggest keeping a copy of the Code of Ethics handy and reading it over once or twice daily. The best way to prepare for this section, like many others, is by practice. This means finding practice questions, whether they are on the CFA Institute's website, a third-party provider, or on Investopedia's quizzer, I highly recommend taking time to answer practice questions often. Doing so will build your ethical intuition. This means that instead of learning the Code and Standards verbatim, you will be able to noodle through, which is a much better game plan. The idea is to build your understanding, not see how much you can regurgitate.

I also suggest you take the recommended procedures in the

Standards seriously because they could be fair game for testing. Know specifics like how long you should keep your record information (Seven years) and keep in mind that fact that when local laws allow insider trading, as a CFA candidate your compliance to the Code and Standards disallows you to engage in insider trading or any other conduct that reflects negatively on the investment profession. Whenever there is a conflict between CFA code and standards and a jurisdiction, the one with the more stringent rules and procedures takes precedence. When claiming to comply with GIPS, any laws that force your firm to deviate from the full-GIPS standard must be disclosed/ explained.

When it comes to GIPS, the best framework I can come up with is Who, What, When, Where, Why and How. To best be prepared to answer GIPS questions, be able to answer these.

Who can claim compliance with GIPS? (Investment firms only; firms should adopt the broadest, most encompassing definition of what a 'firm' means.)

What is GIPS and what do you include? (GIPS are global investment performance standards. All discretionary, fee-paying portfolios must be included in at least one composite.)

What number of periods do you show? (A minimum of *five years* (or *since inception*) and *ten years* after that.)

How are returns calculated and how do you claim compliance? (Remember that dollar-weighting is not allowed because it gives more weight to higher asset portfolios and that compliance requires verification by an *independent third-party*. An internal auditor is **NOT** an independent auditor and therefore, cannot attest that your firm is compliant with the Global Investment Performance Standards.)

If you're in a country in conflict with GIPS, can you still claim compliance? (Yes, but you must disclose and/or explain the nature of the conflict between the local law and the Global Investment Performance Standards.)

Why do we have GIPS? (Firms can distort their past performances and appear to perform better than in actuality by excluding funds that are no longer managed Think about it for a second. If they no longer manage a set of funds, the funds probably did poorly. This form of exclusion is referred to as **survivorship bias**.)

I think that if you can answer those fully and without cheating, you are well prepared for many GIPS questions thrown at you.

I also suggest starting your studying with this topic area and ending your studying with it. That way it'll be fresh in your brain. Although not confirmed, it is said that CFAI looks favorably towards those who excel in the ethics portion of the exam.

Ethics and standards of professional conduct show up on Levels 2 and 3, the subsequent exams should you successful complete Level 1. It is wise to build a solid understanding and foundation here at Level 1, so that when you arrive at the more challenging upper-levels, you won't have to worry as much about this area and you can focus your time and energy on much more mentally-challenging subjects, like Derivatives, which can throw people off and can be the make-it-or-break-it section in determining your passing or failure.

Quantitative Methods

This section's reliance on quantitative reasoning is given away by its meticulously-crafted name. This section is another double-digit percentage of the exam, so it is important to develop a solid understanding. Should you develop a basic framework of how hypothesis testing, probabilities, and distributions work, your ability to intuitively solve problems will be greatly enhanced for this section. Again, there is no replica for practice. Practice, practice, practice! If you still don't understand this section (as I personally found this one of the more difficult sections), I suggest looking up YouTube or Khan Academy videos, or even short Coursera courses, all of which can better explain the process and reasoning and all of which can give you a better chance of passing this section of the exam.

The first subgroup I'll place here is **Yields**. Yields are a measure of return. There are many different yields and they can be add-on or discount. Add-on yields and discount yields may be a new concept to you. The idea is intuitive. An add-on yield is added on to the previous amount and the discount yield is the percentage discount to par (a maturity value).

The primitive yield, and possible most important in building understanding, is the Holding period yield or holding period return.

$$HPY = (P_1 - P_0 + D_1) / P_0$$

Where P_0 is the initial price

D1 is the dividend received

P1 is the price at end of period, or at sale

What you're calculating is the return irrespective of period. In other words, this is NOT an annualized yield.

This can be used to find the EAY (effective annual yield), which makes it annualized and thus comparable to other investment returns.

EAY = (1+HPY)^(365/t) - 1

Where HPY is holding period yield

T is days to maturity

Not to be confused with effective annual rate (EAR), which takes an annual rate and makes it reflect any compounding during the year.

EAR=((1+(i/n))^n) -1

Where i is interest rate

N is the the number of periods per year

The Bond Equivalent Yield is a yield that annualizes the HPY in bond terms (governments use 365 days, whereas banks use 360 day years).

BEY= HPY * (365/t)

Where t is the days to maturity

The money market yield is a yield that compares it to money market securities.

It's similar to the BEY, except it uses 360 instead of 365.

$$MMY = HPY * (360/t)$$

Where t is days to maturity

The previous yields were add-on yields. The next yields are discount yields

Bond Discount Yield

$$BDY = ((PV - Par)/Par)) * (365/t)$$

Where PV is the present value or price paid

Par is the maturity value

T is days to maturity

Bank Discount Yield

$$BDY = ((PV-Par)/Par)) * (360/t)$$

Where PV is present value or price paid

Par is the maturity value

T is the days to maturity

Note that all yield with the world bond in front are 365-day years and all bank/money market yields are 360-day years.

There different types of returns and ways to calculate and average them. A Continuously compounded return is a return that has a compounding period, like quarterly. Think of it as a sort of maximum value.

$$CCR = \ln(p1/po) = \ln(1+HPR)$$

Where p1 is ending value

Po is beginning value

$$HPE = e^{CCR} - 1$$

A weighted return is can be used to determine the expected or actual performance of a portfolio.

$$\text{Expected Return} = W1*R1 + W2*R2$$

W1 is weight of asset1 (how much of the portfolio is asset or asset class 1)

W2 is weight of asset 2

R1 is expected return of asset 1

R2 is expected return of asset 2

Geometric mean returns are the average rate per period returns of multi-period investments.

$$((1+R1)(1+R2)(1+R3))^{\wedge}(1/3) \ -1$$

R = return

Note how it is 1+ R times 1+R... and they are taken to the cubed-root. If it were four returns, it would be all to the (1/4th) power. If there is any variability, this value will be less than the arithmetic mean or simple mean (R1+R2+R3)/3 .

The next subgroup is the Time Value of Money or TVM. Fortunately, a trusty financial calculator like a BAII Plus can calculate a good number of what you will need. Still, understanding what's going on will help you prevent errors in logic and will prevent headaches and guessing games.

$$PV = \frac{FV}{(1+(r/k))^{n*k}}$$

R is the required rate of return

K is the number of periods

N is number of years

Future Value or FV = Present value $(1+(r/k)^{\wedge}(n*k)$

Note the similarities in formula construction. The Present Value is the Future Value discounted by a certain rate of return to the present over some n number of years and k number of periods. The Future Value is the Present Value multiplied by the 1 plus the rate of return to the number of periods and years. This is the value of the investment at some point in the future.

An annuity is a series of payments over years and it can be discounted like an individual payment. Your calculator can value annuities for you or you can discount it via:

$$PV = \text{Cashflow (or Payment)} \left(\frac{1-(1+i)^{-n}}{i} \right)$$

Perpetuities are annuities that go on forever. They can be calculated easily.

$$PVP = Cashflow / Required\ rate\ of\ return$$

This formula helps for PREFERRED STOCK VALUATION.

An annuity due is an annuity that pays at the beginning of the period.

$$\text{PV annuity due} = \text{PV annuity} * (1+(r/k))$$

$$\text{FV annuity due} = \text{FV annuity} * (1+(r/k))$$

The Net Present Value is an important factor in whether or not to accept a project and it is used in capital budgeting. (Corporate finance crossover)

NPV = Initial Outflow + PV of inflows

The rate that makes the NPV = 0 is called the Internal Rate or Return or IRR. If asked about projects of various size, NPV, not IRR, is the critical factor.

The NPV set-up can also help you find the money-weighted rate of return, which would equate to the Internal Rate of

Return that makes the Outflows equal to the cash Inflows.

Probability is an important subgroup that quantifies chance. I suggest reading over Bayes' theorem.

Bayes' = $P(A | B) = (P(B | A) * P(A)) / P(B)$

The (A | B) is read as Probability of A given B

Total Probability states that $P(A) = P(A|B)*P(B) + P(A|B^c)*P(B^c)$

The c means complement or 1 – $P(b)$ = b complement

Addition Rule states that $P(A \text{ or } B) = P(A) + P(B) - P(AB)$

AB means A and B

Multiplication rule states that $P(AB) = P(A|B)*P(B)$

Understanding cumulative and relative frequency are also important. Relative frequency can be thought of as out of all observed values, how often a particularly sought-after value will appear. The cumulative frequency includes all previous values.

Statistical concepts are a major component of this topic area. Having a grasp on this is critical to success in this section.

A key concept here and in other areas of the exam is variance. Variance equates to standard deviation squared. To calculate it is a simple calculation; square the difference between each observed value and the mean, add them together and divide by N for a population or n-1 for a sample.

Covariance is the differences between observed and mean for 1 multiplied by the differences between observed and mean for 2. Divide all this by n-1 for a sample. This gives a measure of the voracity of the correlation between 1 and 2.

An important set of identities to understand, all of which will come back in later readings, is the following set. I cannot stress enough how much knowing the interrelated formulas can help you solve quantitative problems.

Most people have a sense about correlation. If it is negative 1, the two stocks, portfolios, or whatever are inversely correlated. That means that there returns are opposite one another. This is important to understand in portfolio management as managing risk is an important skill of any successful investment professional.

Ordinal scales rank data. Nominal simply categorizes data by a qualitative characteristic, or name. Interval scales place data into bins, ranges, or intervals.

Covariance = Correlation * Standard Deviation(Stock1) * Standard Deviation(Stock2)

      The (stocknumber) is just to label the standard deviations are separate and not identical. An important conclusion is that we can simply divide both sides by the standard deviations and reach our correlation.

Correlation = Covariance / Standard Deviation * Standard Deviation

This comes in handy when dealing with risk-adjusted returns. CAPM, a measure of expected return of a stock with respect to its systematic risk, uses a variable called Beta, which can be calculated as (the covariance of the stock and market) / (Variance of market).

The variance of a two asset portfolio is an important measure to be able to calculate.

Variance of Portfolio = $(w_1^2 * Std.Dev.1^2) + (w_2^2 * std.dev.^2) + 2w_1w_2 Cov_{12}$

Where w1 is weight of stock 1 (proportion of portfolio)

W2 is weight of stock 2

Std.Dev.1 is standard deviation of stock 1

Std. Dev.2 is standard deviation of stock 2

Cov12 is covariance of stocks 1 and 2

Note the first part of the equation sees the weights and standard deviations squared; however, the last part of the equation sees no such squaring. Also, Cov12 could be rewritten as correlation of

1 and 2 times std. dev. Of 1 times std. dev. Of 2.

A measure of dispersion (how spread out the distributions are) is called the coefficient of variation, or the relative standard deviation. This is simply the standard deviation divided by the mean.

A normal distribution is one where 68% lies within -1 standard deviation to 1 standard deviation from the mean. The kurtosis (the relative "height") is 3. Any distribution with a kurtosis of >3 is leptokurtic and anything flatter, or less then 3, is platykurtic.

Standard error of the sample mean equates to the standard deviation divided by the square root of n (where n is the sample size). A sampling error is difference between a sample statistic, like our sample mean, and a population value, like a population mean.

A population is the group to which we are trying to gain some insight. A sample is a selection from the population. Using sampling allows us to make inferences about a larger population.

I suggest reviewing z-tests, t-tests, chi-square and F-tests. Know what these are testing, why they're used and how to calculate the test statistic and determine whether or not to reject the null hypothesis relative to some critical value. The below is by no means an easy way out, but this basic understanding should help in how you go about solving problems.

A z-test is typically used when variance is known and you have a large sample (>30). T-tests are for smaller data sets. The Chi-square distribution is skewed and shows a distribution of variances from repeated trials. F-test

F-statistic= $S2^2 / S1^2$ where s1 is std. dev. Of , s2 is std. dev. Of 2

A z-score indicated how many standard deviations the value is from the population mean. It's simple the observed value minus the mean and then divide by the standard deviation.

A z-test statistic is (observed minus mean)/(std.dev / sqrt of n)

Sqrt is square root

Keep in mind that the denominator is the same as the standard error,

A t-statistic is calculated the same, except that instead of using population measures, sample measures are used.

I suggest understanding that with a positively skewed distribution the mean is greater than the median, which is greater than the mode. The opposite is true for a negatively skewed distribution.

Constructing a confidence interval is done by taking the mean value +/- Reliability factor * (std.dev./ sqrt of n)

Or simply, the mean plus or minus a reliability factor times the standard error.

A binomial distribution occurs when you have x successes in n trials, where each has the same probability as the last. Fortunately, the financial calculator can do this for us calculation-wise, but it is wise to understand it and be able to calculate it should your mental functioning on exam day hinder your ability to recall the calculator function.

nCx (called n choose x) = n! / (x! (nix)!)

! = factorial; it means you multiply that number by each of the preceding numbers, so for 3!, 3*2*1, or 6.

The Sharpe Ratio is (the return of the portfolio minus the risk-free rate) / std. dev. Of the portfolio

It's a return over risk measure. It relates to the Capital Allocation line or

CAL, which looks at total risk. The Security market line, or SML, relates to systematic risk and uses beta in place of std. dev. (which is called the traynor ratio). M2 is the alpha or excess return on the CAL and Jensen's Alpha is the excess return on the SML (Portfolio return minus CAPM).

The Safety-first ratio is the (return(of the portfolio) minus a return threshold) / std. dev. Of the portfolio.

Economics

Economics is an important area, as it relates to the underlying forces driving the markets. This includes but is not limited to Supply and Demand, Monetary Policy and Gross Domestic Product. I will begin with foreign exchange, since it relates to interest rates and the supply of money. I think starting here will help you build an understanding. If it is not making sense, you may wish to skip ahead and come back to this after you have some basics down.

The first term I'll introduce is a primal one. That means that if you get this, you can pretty much understand the rest of the reading. The idea is that markets allign to form an equilibrium price and when that price is below the equilibrium or expected price, there is money to be made in arbitrage (simultaneously buying it in one market and selling it in another). Arbitrage helps to bridge the gap and bring prices towards equilibrium. Thus, Power Purchasing Parity is an ideal concept to embark with. PPP states basically that if I have one item in one country trading at a dollar and in another country, that same item is fifty cents, the exchange rate should ideally reflect this difference. That is to say that for every dollar the first country trades in exchange for country 2's currency, it should be given $.50. This never comes out to be always true, or even mostly true. This is just an ideal sense of what one country's money can buy versus another's.

Exchange rate = (Price of good x in country 1) / (price of good x in country 2)

The spot rate is simply the exchange rate at a set point in time. The forward rate, the rate at which an exchange will be made at a future date, can be calculated as the spot rate * (1+if / 1+Id), where if is interest rate of the foreign country and id is the interest rate of the domestic country.

The real exchange rate is the (nominal exchange rate * domestic inflation)/ foreign inflation. This adjusts for inflation in both economies. This concept applied to a fixed basket or index is called the real effective exchange rate.

Bps (or bips) are used a lot. It means .01%, or think of it as 1/100th of 1%.

The following information presented will now be relative to non-foreign-exchange -related economics, including both macroeconomics and microeconomics. Supply is how much of a good people are willing and able to provide at a given price; since price is on the y-axis, supply is upward sloping because at an infinite price, I will supply an infinite amount and at zero, I will produce none. Demand is how much someone is willing and able to buy at a given price. This is downward sloping because quantity is on the x-axis and at an infinite price, none will be bought, but at a price of zero, demand is infinite. As I would expect most to know, land, labor, capital and entrepreneurship are the factors of production.

The Fisher Effect states that the real interest rate is equal to the nominal interest rate minus expect inflation.

The GDP equation is Y = Consumption + Investment+Government Spending+(Exports-Imports)

Investment means private investment in factors of production, not in securities like stocks and bonds. That is a common misunderstanding and I hope you realize that purchasing a security does not materially affect GDP (goods produced), whereas building a factory most likely would.

The price elasticity of demand is the % change in quantity demanded divided by the % change in price. The percent change is ending value minus beginning and that answer divided by ((ending + beginning)/2) – this is the average of the two. Think of it like a balance sheet, which is fixed at a given point in time. The average between two balance sheets is used for ratios that involve income statement items since income statements are continuous are reflect a whole period.

The cross-price elasticity of demand is the same equation, except this time the % change in price is the change in price for another product. If the quantity sold of our product goes up when the price of another product goes up, they are said to be substitutes. When another product's prices are up and our product's sales decline, they are complements. Think about Peanut butter and jelly. If jelly's price goes up, less people will buy peanut butter and vice-versa.

The income elasticity of demand is the % change in Quantity divided by the percent change in income. Remember that the change in income can be negative. If people desire your product when they are poor and will not touch it when they are richer, your good is said to be inferior. Think ramen noodles. I doubt anyone with a six-figure salary buys such a product; however, college kids on a budget can't get enough of them.

These elasticities can be applied to supply. Just make sure you are not using quantity demanded for supply calculations and vice-versa.

Interestingly, there are goods that see higher demand as prices rise. If price is the only thing that affects demand, they are said to be Giffen goods. If they are bought for status, or as Thorstein Veblan wrote "conspicuous consumption", they are Veblan goods.

Now on to Costs. Total cost is equal to total fixed costs plus total variable costs. In the short-run, if a firm is covering its TVC, it should keep operating. In the long-run, perfectly competitive industries' firms will not have an economic profit. They may have an accounting profit in the short-run. In perfect competition, products are undifferentiated, there are no entry or exit barriers, and many competitors. In monopolistic competition, firms have differentiated product offerings. In monopolies, there's one supplier. Just because there is one supplier does not mean they can charge whatever they want, especially if demand is elastic. Oligopolies can act like cartels and collude and according to game theory, they will act within their own best interests and not break any arrangements with their partners if they make sense. I suggest reading more into these types of competitions and how they work.

Marginal cost is equal to the change in total cost divided by the change in quantity. Average fixed cost is total fixed cost divided by the quantity. Average Variable cost is total variable cost divided by the quantity. Average total cost is total cost divided by quantity or the average fixed cost plus the average variable cost.

Unemployment rates are calculated as the number of unemployed divided by the labor force and this times 100. Labor force means anyone working or actively seeking employment. Labor force participation rate is the labor force divided by the working-age population and this times 100. This tells you out of everyone who could be in the labor force, what percentage actually are. LFPR is important because unemployment could be going down due to simply the labor force getting smaller.

Employment to population rate determines the percentage of the WAP that is employed. Take the number of employed divided by the working age population and multiply this by 100.

Indices are important to consider. CPI or consumer price index is commonly used and the underlying principles can be used for other indices if you get stuck. The inflation rate under this method is simply the difference between the current CPI and last year's CPI divided by last year's CPI.

It's simply the current cost of the basket of goods divided by the base year cost of the same basket of goods and multiplied by 100.

Real GDP is simply a measure of how many products were produced, regardless of price. GDP deflator is nominal GDP divided by real GDP and then multiplied by 100. GDP is equal to aggregate demand.

The potential deposit multiplier looks at how much money is created within a given bank, by its ability to loan funds. It is simply 1 divided by the required reserve percentage. The required reserve percentage or ratio is the amount that must be kept in cash at the bank should depositors require their funds and allows for liquidity.

This multiplier multiplied by the increase in excess reserves will tell you the maximum or potential increase in the supply of money.

The money multiplier is the same as the potential deposit multiplier except both the numerator and denominator are reduced by the amount of cash held in hand by people (measured as a ratio of deposits). The change in the quantity of money supplied is the monetary base (what the Fed Reserve puts out) times the money multiplier.

The velocity of money is the amount of transactions for which a given unit of currency is used in a given year. It tends to be static over time within a country, but can vary widely from region to region. This velocity times the money supply gives us GDP, which is essentially the price of goods times the quantity of goods. This can be transformed to solve for price, quantity, etc.

I suggest being able to interpret slope (rise over run), quantity and price relationships, and understanding taxation, tariffs, subsidies, and quotas and how they affect surplus and prices.

Financial Reporting and Analysis

Assets are equal to Liabilities plus Equity. Assets and liabilities are made up of current and non-current portions. Equity is made up of Contributed Capital and Retained Earnings (which is cumulative net income minus dividends). Current year Retained Earnings is equal to Net income minus dividends or Net income times the retention rate, which is 1 – dividend payout rate. Dividend payout rates tell us how much of net income is coming back to us in the form of a dividend. The growth rate of dividends is equal to Return on Equity times the retention rate.

A stock can be valued using its dividends. The next dividend, which is the last dividend times 1 + the growth rate as a decimal, divided by the required rate in decimals plus 1 to the n number of periods. If the dividend is expected to grow perpetually, the PV of a growing perpetuity will work. Take the dividend and divide it by the required return minus the growth rate. A preferred stock can be valued as a typical perpetuity, the dividend per share divided by the required rate.

The DuPont identity is important to understand because it can be used to help you solve a number of problems. It is an identity used to calculate the ROE.

ROE=(Net Income/ Equity)= (Net income/sales)(sales/total assets)(total assets/ equity)

In order, ^Net profit margin ^total asset turnover ^assets-to-equity (debt) ratio

The operating is cycle is how long it takes to turn a good into cash after it is received. So, DOH+DSO or days on hand plus days sales outstanding. DOH is 365/(cogs/avg. inventory) and DSO is 365/(sales/avg. acct. receivables). The net operating cycle or cash conversion cycle includes the payments to suppliers.

DOH+DSO−DPO= cash conversion cycle. DPO is 365/(cogs (include any other purchases if info is available)/avg. acct. payables).

Operating cash flow is net income plus depreciation, or sales minus costs minus taxes. Net capital spending is ending fixed assets minus beginning fixed assets plus depreciation. Changes in net working capital = ending − beginning. (Net working capital is current assets minus current liabilities). The working capital ratio is current assets over current liabilities. Quick ratio excludes inventory from current assets and cash ratio is only cash and cash equivalents over liabilities.

Cash flow from assets = cash flow to creditors plus cash flow to stockholders = operating cash flow − net capital spending − changes in net working capital

Cash flow to creditors is interest paid − net new borrowing = interest paid − (ending debt − beginning debt)

Cash flow to stockholders is dividends paid – net new equity raised

Financial leverage = ROE/ROA = (EBIT/ EBIT minus interest)

Operating leverage= (sales-tvc)/ (sales-tvc-tfc)

Total debt ratio=(assets-equity)/(assets)

Debt-to-equity = debt/ equity

Cash coverage = (EBIT + depreciation)/interest expense

Times interest earned = EBIT/ interest expense

Capital intensity = total assets/sales

Price-to-earnings = Stock price divided by EPS

Price-to-sales = market capitalization / sales

Market cap = share price * shares outstanding

Price to book = stock price/ book value per share

It's important here to not only know formulas, but to understand the nuances of IFRS and US GAAP. Unfortunately, if you studied GAAP, you'll have to learn some IFRS and be able to decipher the two.

The EPS or earnings per share is equal to Net Income, which is after-tax earnings, minus preferred share dividends and all this divided by the weighted average of common shares outstanding. These are time-weighted meaning that if there were 100,000 shares outstanding all year and 50,000 were issued the first of June, the weighted average would be 125,000, or 100,000(12/12)+50,000(6/12).

Diluted EPS takes into account any dilutive, not antidilutive, securities. Antidilutive securities would raise EPS and dilutive securities lower it. If you have convertible preferred, simply don't subtract their dividends from net income and calculate the weighted average. If you have debt, take the after-tax interest expense and add it to net income, which should be divided by your new weighted average of shares. To test for dilution, simply divide the expenses of said security by the number of shares it would create. If it's less than basic EPS, it is in fact dilutive.

Treasury stock method assumes a co uses proceeds from options to buy shares at avg. mkt price. So New shares is equal to (Average stock price – exercise price)/avg. price, all of which is multiplied by the shares of the options.

Cash return on equity = Operating cash flow / Avg. Equity

Cash flow per share = (OCF − preferred dividends)/ shares outstanding

Fixed charge coverage = (EBIT+Lease payments)/(interest payments+lease payments)

Free cash flow to equity= OCF -NCS+Net new borrowing

Current cost of inventory(FIFO) = Inventory under LIFO+LIFO reserve

COGS(FIFO)= LIFOcogs-change in LIFOreserve

Net Income(FIFO)= LIFOnet income+(after tax LIFO reserve change)

Straight-line depreciation =(book value-salvage)/useful years

Inventories include transporting, reworking, etc. to get it to its final state. No storage of finished goods, admin. Overheads, or abnormal wastes are inventory values.

Double-declining = 2/ useful life *(book value after accumulated depreciation)

Income tax expense= taxes paybles+DTL or minus DTA

The bulk of the exam is this section, so spend a lot of time here if you are not comfortable.

Corporate Finance

Earlier, I introduced Net Present Value and IRR. Please refer to the Quantitative Methods section of this material if you are not yet familiar or comfortable with those terms and what they mean.

Corporate Finance is mostly about capital budgeting, determining required rates of return, and projects.

The payback period for a project is the amount of time it takes to recover the initial investment. Count the years by subtracting from the investment the cashflows each year. When you get to a year where you have some investment left, but not enough to cover the full year, take the unrecovered cost and divide it by the cash flow of that year to get a partial year.

The profitability index is the present value of the future cash flows divided by the initial investment.

Average Accounting rate of return is the average net income divided by the average book value.

Earlier on, in Quantitative Methods, we discussed Beta and said how Beta is the covariance of the stock and market divided by the variance of the market. In this section, we are going to be applying Beta. Beta is a measure of systematic risk and is vital to calculating required returns on stocks and projects.

The Capital Asset Pricing Model = Expected Return = Risk-free rate + Beta *(Return on market – risk-free rate)

(Return on market – risk-free rate) is known as the market risk premium. The amount of return expected by putting money in a riskier security than the risk-free rate.

Two other ways to do cost equity include bond-yield-plus-premium, which is essentially what it says, and D1/Po +g, essentially dividend yield times the growth rate.

If we are getting into a project that will have a different operating activity than the majority of our firm, using our beta gives us an incorrect measure. Take the levered beta (equity beta) and divide is by 1+ the after tax debt-to-equity ratio for a pureplay company in that operating activity. We can then relever it to our capital structure by multiplying that by 1+the after tax debt-to-equity ratio for our company.

WACC or the weighted average cost of capital finds the weighted average return for all capital sources for the firm.

WACC= weight of equity times cost of equity(usually CAPM) + Weight of preferred*(preferred dividend over preferred price)+weight of debt*(after-tax interest expense/ market value of debt)

The market premium for a developing country includes a country-specific risk. This is called the country risk premium and is calculated by taking the sovereign yield spread * (std. dv. Equity / std. dev. Debt).

Portfolio Management

This section includes readings from Quantitative Methods and Corporate Finance. Look over those sections, specifically variance of 2-asset portfolio, CAPM, correlation, and the SML/CAL differentiation.

The expected return on a portfolio can be written ass the sums of probabilities of the economy in a given state times the returns of the assets given those states.

Variance of returns measures volatility of the asset. This is the sums of the probability of the economy in a given state * the squared differences between the returns if the economy is in a given state minus the expected return.

The covariance is the sum of the probabilities of the economy in a given state * the difference between the return of asset 1 in state of economy*the difference between the return of asset 2 in state of economy.

A sample covariance is the difference between return of 1 at a time and mean return times the difference between return of 2 at a time and mean return, with all being divided by n-1.

Correlation can be calculated as previously written.

The expected return can be seen as a sum of the weights of each asset times their individual expected returns. The standard deviation of a portfolio is the square root of the variance, which was shown earlier in Quantitative Methods.

Expected return, with respect to risk, can be calculated as the risk-free fate + std. dev. Of portfolio *((expected return − risk-free rate)/standard dev. Of market).

Total risk is unsystematic (many specific risks to the industry or co.) and systematic risk (beta). Beta calculations were covered in Quantitative Methods and Corporate Finance.

In zero-beta CAPM, simply replace the risk-free rate with the expected return on a zero-beta portfolio. Zero-beta means its returns are not correlated to market returns.

Equity Instruments

Equity valuations techniques were introduced here in Corporate Finance. As you can tell by now, there is a lot of overlap in the material and that should help better your understanding. Instead of going back over dividend discount model

One way to find the intrinsic value of a stock is to calculate a P/E ratio by taking the dividend payout ratio and dividing it by the required rate minus the growth rate. If we say 'trailing', that refers to the past. If we say 'leading', that means expected in the future.

If you bought stock o margin, the trigger price for a margin call would be the price of the security times (1 – initial margin / 1- maintenance margin).

A price-weighted index says we'll have the same number of shares of each company. Bigger share prices means higher weights. Equal weighted mean that each return is equally weighted, so that share prices and share counts are meaningless essentially. Fundamental weighting gives more weight to stocks based on their book value or other value metrics. Market-value weighted is based on market-cap. If the number of shares outstandingequate, it's likely market-cap and price will be equal.

Also, I do suggest going over some technical analysis as questions on these show up often in practice quizzes.

Fixed Income

Full price is the price paid plus any accrued interest. Accrued interest is the amount of interest earned between payments.

Durations measure the change in the value of a bond. It's simply the change in value over the change in yield. The Macaulay duration is were the reinvestment risk equals the liquidity risk.

It's based on weighting the years based on their contribution to the total PV of the bond.

High-yield bonds have a higher risk associated with them called default risk. To account for this, there is a credit spread, or a default risk premium, which varies depending on the grade of the bond, etc.

Absolute yield spread in the difference in yield between a higher-yield and lower-yield bond. By dividing this by the yield on the benchmark, we get a relative yield spread. The yield of a given bond divided by the benchmark's is called a yield ratio.

Callable bonds must be the value of an option-free bond minus the call option. Calls reduce price appreciation because no one would pay at or above the call value.

Putable bonds are more desirable to bondholders because they reserve the right to sell the bond back to the issuer at a pre-determined price. All else equal, a putable bond will have a shorter duration than an equivalent option-free bond.

Bond prices are equal to the PV of their future cash flows and can be calculated using a financial calculator. A zero coupon bond is simply worth the discounted par value. The current yield is an annual yield that takes the annualized coupon payment and divides it by the bond price. Premium bonds will have a negative capital gains yield and discount bonds will have a positive capital gains yield. The treatment of this capital appreciation can vary.

TIPS are inflation protected. The coupon payments made semi-annually reflect an inflation-adjusted par value.

A spot rate can be found by taking the geometric mean of the forward rates.

The 1-year forward rate two years from now is (1 plus the 3 year spot rate)^3/(1+two year spot rate)^2 -1.

Effective duration is the price with yield down minus price with yield up, divided by 2 times initial price times the change in yield.

The value of a basis point is the average of the change in bp when up and change when bp is down.

Derivatives

Derivatives is a long dreaded part of the curriculum. It's only introduced at

Level 1 and honestly it's not that bad. Just remember the put-call parity. That is that a fiduciary call is equal to a protective put.

A call can be worth the price of the underlying minus the exercise price if it's in the money. If not, it is worthless. A call is an option to buy at a certain price. If I have an option to buy 1 share at $2 and the stock is at $4, I'm in the money and if I cash it, I profit $2.

A covered call is when you own the asset and write a call. You net the premium against the cost basis and if it does get cashed, you get the difference between the call exercise price and the adjusted cost basis.

A put can be worth the exercise minus the underlying or it can be zero. Remember a put is the option to sell at a certain price.

For European calls and puts, the exercise price must be discounted by the risk-free rate over the remaining time to expiry. That's because you cannot exercise a European call or put until expiry. American puts and calls can be exercised prior. Therefore, an American call or put must be at least equal to the European equivalent.

An interest rate swap is where you agree to pay a variable rate and the other party pays a fixed amount. These are netted.

Option values have an intrinsic element and a time element.

Alternative Investments

Remember that alternatives can be good for diversification, but they do tend to have overstated returns and understated variance.

Remember that commodities have a convenience yield. Normally, the convenience yield is low and we are in contango (upward sloping), but if it is high, we are in backwardation (downward sloping). Convenience yield simply means the desire to have the commodity in physical form.

A roll yield occurs in futures markets that are experiencing backwardation. The roll yield is the return made by switching from a short-term to a longer-term contract, since the future will gain value as expiration becomes closer. The traders profit when futures converge towards spot price appreciation. There is a major issue with this type of trading and that is that a shift from backwardation to contango can cause significant losses and can be hard to be predict for the experienced and inexperienced alike.

Hedge funds charge a 2 and 20, meaning two percent of assets under management (end of year or beginning) and 20% of the return past a hurdle rate (this could be all inclusive or not and is usually net of the management fee). If it is inclusive, that means there's a soft hurdle. If it only takes its performance fee from what's in excess of the hurdle rate, that is a hard hurdle rate.

Real estate value can be assessed as NOI/ r , which can be expanded as (potential income less any vacancy or bad debt – taxes – maintenance and other expenses)/ required rate of return.

There's a gain if the proceeds of a sale exceed book value (after depreciation).

Remember that Venture Capital expects a larger percentage of failure, but the ones that do succeed pay off very well (the next Google if you will).

I hope this guide helps you as you prepare to take the daunting exam. Remember to do as many practices and mocks as you can.

Thanks for reading- Josh

Printed in Great Britain
by Amazon